DENES AG...

SONGS TO REMEMBER

POPULAR — INSPIRATIONAL — CONCERT

Yorktown Music Press, Inc.
New York/London/Paris/Sydney/Tokyo/Copenhagen/Madrid

Order No. YK 21923
International Standard Book Number: 0.8256.8109.X

Exclusive Distributors:
Music Sales Corporation
257 Park Avenue South, New York, NY 10010 USA
Music Sales Limited
8/9 Frith Street, London W1D 3JB England
Music Sales Pty. Limited
120 Rothschild Street, Rosebery, Sydney, NSW 2018, Australia

Printed in the United States of America

CONTENTS

FOREWORD

THIS collection of songs, representing largely an early phase of my creative activities, is offered here not only as a musical reminiscence and a nostalgic retrospect but also as a still valid, effective vocal performing repertory.

Some of these melodies were written by me years ago, others are of a much more recent vintage, penned for the stage, radio and allied media, frequently recorded and performed. A few of the earliest entries credit three writers (including me), originating from my beginning days on Broadway, when such associations were quite common practice, dictated by or deemed advantageous by the highly competitive rush for success on Tin Pan Alley.

In the original releases these songs were published in separate sheet music form. It gives me great pleasure and satisfaction to make them available here in one volume for a pleasant, diverting journey through my varied melodic landscape and for a handy source of effective program material to entertain and/or inspire audiences.

Denes Agay
August 2001

When I Come Home Again

from the Army musical "Johnny Get Your Fun"

Words by
Brent Gunts and George Herz

Music by
Denes Agay

I'm Hap-Hap-Happy in Love

Theme song from the radio show "Guest Star"

Words by
Brent Gunts and George Herz

Music by
Denes Agay

Brightly

Chorus

It's "good - bye" —— to my blues song, —— For I'm set now ——

—— with a new song, —— Mis - ter Mis - 'ry, look out, —— It's

my day to shout, —— I'm hap - hap - hap - py in love ———————— Sing

"Heigh - ho," —— see my feet dance, —— Hear my heart beat ——

No One's Heart

from the musical play "My Romance"

Words by
Fred Jay and Irving Reid

Music by
Denes Agay

Magic Moment

From the musical play "My Romance"

Words by
Rowland Leigh

Music by
Denes Agay

Moments like this of wonderful bliss Are precious and all too few. Let

us not allow This moment somehow to melt as the morning dew.

Moderately with, expression

Chorus

In a mag - ic mo - ment both our hearts were swept a - way

Some - thing won - der - ful and strange is in the air.

And our mag - ic mo - ment's not to - mor - row but to - day

Was It Make Believe

(Faites-Vous Semblant)
Paroles francaises de Bernard Hilda

Words by
Milton Leeds

Music by
Denes Agay

24

Tell Me

Was It a Dream?

Words by
Frank Leigh

Music by
Denes Agay

Infatuation

Words by
Carol Woodberry

Music by
Denes Agay

If this is love there should be mus - ic,

The sweet - est song you ev - er heard, If you can't hear it

don't call it love, In - fat - u - a - tion is the word.

If this is love there should be laugh - ter,_____

The Loneliness Won't Leave

Words by
Earl Shuman

Music by
Denes Agay

Willie, The Whistling Whale

Words by
Lewis Allen

Music by
Denes Agay

Whale, Wil-lie, the Whis-tling Whale, The peo-ple all gath-er from

shore to shore,___ They laugh and they clap and they hol-ler for more:___

(Intro. to optional 2nd Chorus)

2nd Chorus Willie, the Whistling Whale
Willie, the Whistling Whale,
He twists all needles
In the compass box
He turns every rudder
And upsets the clocks.

Willie, the Whistling Whale,
Willie, the Whistling Whale,
He flips his flippers,
His tail goes thump,
He makes the skippers
On the big boats jump.

The Statue of Liberty heard his song
And gave him a friendly glance,
He whistled loud and he whistled long
And suddenly she began to dance.

to Coda ⊕

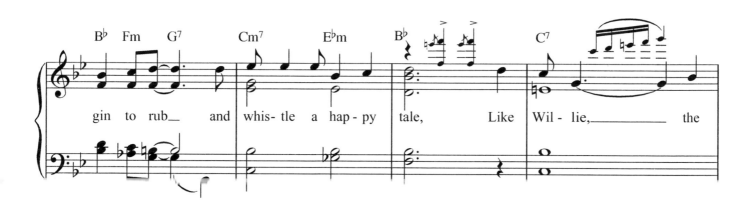

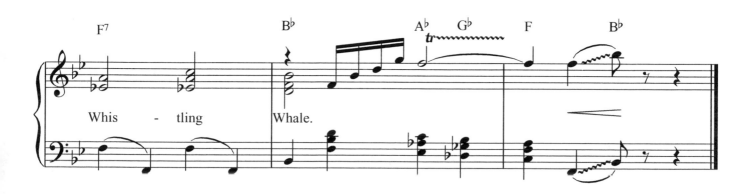

A New Shade of Blue

Words by
Denes Agay and Brent Gunts

Music by
Denes Agay

41

42

If You Wait

(Tango d'Amour)

Words by
Earl Shuman

Music by
Denes Agay

Moderate, marked beat

Wait for the sun, If you wait for the sun, Then the day goes by;

Wait for the rain, If you wait for the rain, Then the well runs dry;

Wait for the rose, If you wait for the rose, Then the win - ter comes;____ And if you should

wait for the cake, that's a mis - take, You're left,____ with on - ly crumbs.

45

Chanson à la Russe

Words and Music by
Denes Agay

Hope you'll al-ways be, Nev-er for-get-ting what you mean to me.

Oh_____ Oh_____ Nev-er for-get-ting what you mean to me.

How Well I Remember

Words and Music by
Denes Agay

How Much Wood Would a Woodchuck Chuck

(If a Wood-Chuck Would Chuck Wood?)

Words by
Walter Hirsch

Music by
Denes Agay and Emery H. Heim

52

When My Ship Comes Sailing Home Again

Words by
Walter Hirsch

Music by
Denes Agay and Emery H. Heim

55

56

Down the Gypsy Trail

from the Motion Picture "Ecstasy"

Words by
Walter Hirsch

Music by
Denes Agay and Emery H. Heim

Lullaby Bay

Words and Music by
Jimmy Eaton, Denes Agay
and Larry Wagner

1. Come sail-or lad-die, to bed-dy come lad-die, Mom-my and Dad-dy
2. Dream lit-tle skip-per, a-sail in your clip-per, ov-er the dip-per

near you will stay till you are har-bored where dream boats are har-bored
dreams will come true safe on an o-cean of love and de-vo-tion

Cheer Up

(For the Best Is Yet to Come)
Theme song of the British-American Ambulance Corps

Words by
Lou Lawrence

Music by
Denes Agay and Emery H. Heim

In old Ti-bet the peo-ple don't hur-ry They live a cen-tu-ry right through_____ They have an an-ti-dote for

Strange Are the Ways of Love

from the musical "Starlight Serenade"

Words by
Fred Jay and Irving Reid

Music by
Denes Agay

day._____ I feel like a hat that was

stepped up-on and light-ly thrown a - way.

rit. . . . .

Rather slow

Chorus

Strange are the ways of love;_____ But then

p espressivo

who would try to rea-son why we love at all._____

You think you are so free, free as a star. But stars al-so

tum-ble and fall._____ How

strange what a love can do,_____ More than

one has tried to hold its tide, but all in vain;_____

You can't run a - way, you can't sub - due it,

you're bound to it witch - craft or spell, Hea - ven or Hell,

Strange are the ways of love. I

parlando

can't see my way in the dark, and yet I must make this ad - miss - ion I'm

more than will - ing to em - bark   on an al - most hope - less

miss - ion,   on an al - most hope - less miss - ion.

Coda

ways   of   love;

tenderly   *ten.*

Strange are the ways of   love.

Too Soon

from the musical "Starlight Serenade"

Words by
Fred Jay and Irving Reid

Music by
Denes Agay

Too soon will this beau-ti-ful night be a mem-o-ry._____ Much too

soon will this new love be part of what used to be._____ So let's take our to-

night and make it last for us,_____ Though no to - mor - row is in sight there'll be a

past for us._____ Too soon will the break-ing of dawn mean good- bye, my love____

____ The wan - ing moon soon will leave us and then so must I, my love._____

____ So let's pre - tend that these mo - ments are ne - ver to end, and as

long as there still is a moon___ say you love me, it can't be_ Too Soon.___

Oh, how I wish that nights like this would last for - ev - er; Yes, for - ev - er,

leave us nev - er. Hold back the hands of time and make this mo - ment lin - ger, till all fires are

burned to cin - der, then___ I'd hold you near___ and I would

If Hearts Could Speak

from the musical "Starlight Serenade"

Words by
Fred Jay and Irving Reid

Music by
Denes Agay

But hearts don't speak and so you've no way to know just what I feel and yet con-ceal. I would-n't have to cling to words that are weak,___ I'd win your heart if hearts could speak.

You Won't Know Happiness

(Unless You Give It)

from the musical "Starlight Serenade"

Words by
Fred Jay and Irving Reid

Music by
Denes Agay

2. Should you be wond'ring
Just why you are sad
Why all the things you do
So often go wrong.

Don't keep wond'ring
Cause the trouble you've had
Are the selfish little schemes
You've kept too long.

have to reach for e - lu - sive stars in the sky._____ It's what you give and share_____

_____ and not the tak - king,_____ The dreams you're mak - ing_____ de - pend on

you. In giv - ing hap - pi - ness you'll find your

Starlight Serenade

from the musical "Starlight Serenade"

Words by
Fred Jay and Irving Reid

Music by
Denes Agay

Here am I the night and I caught in wish - ful dreams of

spring. Here am I 'twixt earth and sky, Do you hear me sing,

With a slow lilt

Chorus

Do you hear me sing _____ Night - in - gales in wil - low

poco rit. . . . . . .

mp

a tempo

trees hear my star - light se - re - nade. _____ Riv - ers rol - ling to the

piu animato *a tempo*

seas hear my song be - ing played. _____ There is mu - sic

mf

As of Today

from the musical "Starlight Serenade"

Words by
Fred Jay and Irving Reid

Music by
Denes Agay

gone, a gold-en dawn fills the air with a song,_____ with a won-der-ful

song._____ *Chorus* As of to-day,_____ as of to-day,_____

____ There's a great big fu-ture on its way._____ So reach out and

get your share of it,____ Help your-self to all that's there of it.____

The time,_____ The time is now,_____ There are fields of hap-pi-ness to plow,_____ from now on the sun is here to stay,_____ _____ Dreams are bloom-in' for ev'-ry hu-man for-ev-er,____ ____ as of to-day!_____

Believing

Recorded by Rose Bampton

Words by
Fred Jay and Irving Reid

Medium Voice

Music by
Denes Agay

lieve, Your faith will see you through. Through dark - ness_____ When there is

no one by your side To tell you_____ just where you are; At

cross - roads_____ with just your lone - ly heart to guide, A pray'r_____ can take you

far. Be - liev - ing, It's your be - liev - ing That lights the way for you When hope is all but gone; So with-out fear go on and on Be - liev - ing.

We're Making the World
A Better World

Words by
Nelson Cogane

Music by
Denes Agay

for my daughter on her 17th birthday

Old Irish Blessing

Traditional

Music by
Denes Agay

Calmly, with warmth

mp

p May the road rise to

mp dim. *p*

Bm

meet you, May the wind be al-ways at your back.

G F#m

mf The

mf

Bm A G | Bm A D | Bm A G

sun shine warm up-on your face. The rains fall soft___ up-

p

dim. *p*

Our Hearts Are Full of Song

Words by
Nelson Cogane

Music by
Denes Agay

mel - o - dy can flow, Then hap - pi - ness can grow And lead us to a bright - er

cresc. sempre

poco rit.   *a tempo*

day,   Yes, lead us to a bright - er day!_____ *f* Our

crescendo.

poco rit.   *a tempo*

hearts are full of joy, Let us share it, Let's de - clare it, With a

For You My Love

(Solo or Duet)

Words by
Sidney Leif

Music by
Denes Agay

The Yankee Peddler

Words by
Sidney Leif

Music by
Denes Agay

fan-cy cop-per warm-in' pan, Or store bought-en clothes, _____ The

Yan-kee Ped-dler's on his way, I seen his cart to-day, It's paint-ed red to match his

Fast (♩ = 126)

nose. _____ One and all, _____

Hear his call: _____

rit . . . . molto . . . .

Gaily, with a carefree lilt *(not fast)*

Doo - dle - de - doo, doo - dle - de - doo, I'm

Like a guitar

sell - in' you stuff that is al - most bran' new.

cresc.

Doo - dle - de - done, doo - dle - de -

poco rit

poco rit

done, Got more things than ev - er growed un - der the

a tempo

rit

o - ver we'll all have some fun, _____ When

Broaden *very broad* Tempo I°

trad - in' is o - ver we'll all have some fun! _____

Duet in Waltz Time

Male and Female Voice

Words and Music by
Denes Agay

Dream While You May

An Aria In Waltz Time

Words by
Jean Reynolds Davis

Music by
Denes Agay

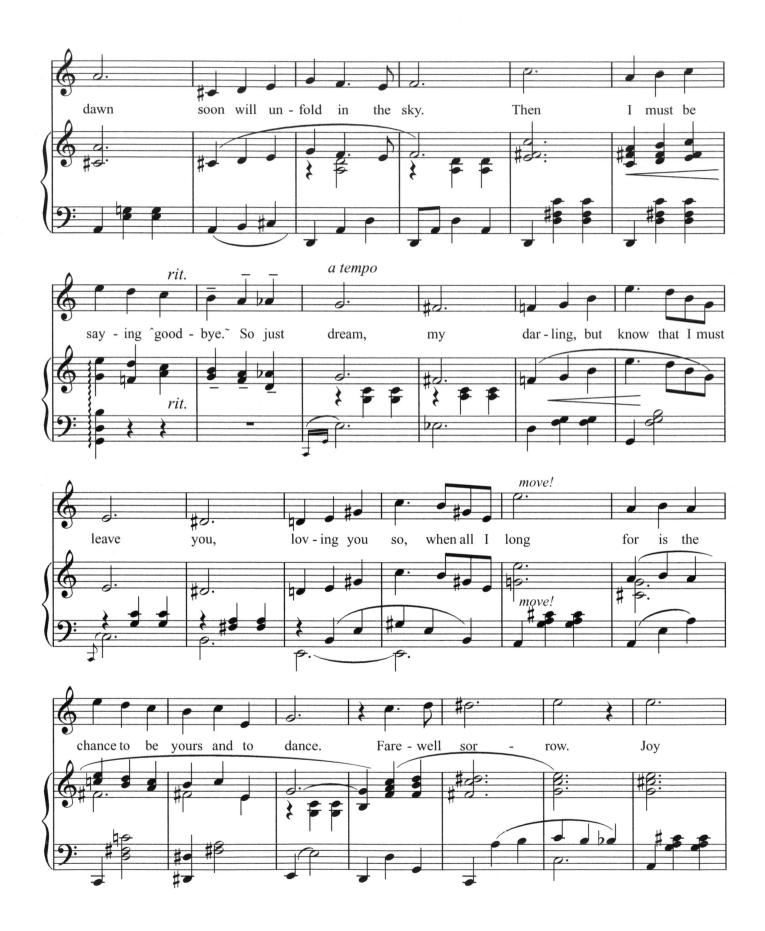

dawn soon will un-fold in the sky. Then I must be

rit. — — *a tempo*

say-ing ˆgood - bye.˜ So just dream, my dar-ling, but know that I must

rit.

move!

leave you, lov-ing you so, when all I long for is the

move!

chance to be yours and to dance. Fare-well sor - row. Joy

Mexican Serenade

Poem by
Arthur Guiterman

Music by
Denes Agay

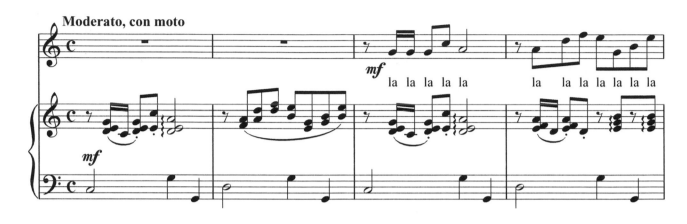

la la la la la   la   la la la la la la

la la la la la   la   When the lit - tle ar - ma - dil - lo With his head up - on his pil - low

Sweet - ly rests,   la la la la la And the par - ra - keet and lin - do Flit - ting

pon-der, ev-er fon-der, Dear, of you,_____ dear, of you!

la la la la la   la   la la la la la la   la la la la la._____

f May no rev-o-lu-tion shock you, May the earth-quake gent-ly rock you To re-

pose,_____ While the sen-ti-men-tal pan-thers Sniff the

pol - len - lad - en an - thers of the rose!_____ While the

pel - i - can is pin - ing, While the moon is soft - ly shin - ing On the stream,___

_____ May the song that I am sing - ing Send a ten - der ca - dence wing - ing Through your

dream!_____ I have just one wish to ut - ter That you

126

The First Psalm
(Vocal Duet)

Words Traditional

Music by Denes Agay

Fast, with a driving rhythm

all that he does he pros - pers,_____

in all that he does he pros - pers

Fast, with a driving rhythm

The wick - ed are not so, the

The wick - ed are not so, the

wick - ed are not so, but are like the chaff_____which the

wick - ed are not so, but are like the chaff_____ which the

poco rit.　　　　a tempo

The way of the wick - ed____ will per - ish!_____

poco rit.　　　　a tempo

mf cresc.

Ah_____

mf cresc.

Ah_____

f rit.

f

rit.

precipitando

136